Little Book of
WILDFLOWERS IN SILK RIBBON

Jenny Bradford

SALLY MILNER PUBLISHING
(MILNER CRAFT SERIES)

First published in 1999 by

Sally Milner Publishing Pty Ltd

1423 Burra Road

Burra Creek 2620

Australia

© Jenny & Don Bradford, 1999

Design by Anna Warren, Warren Ventures, Sydney

Photography by John Tucker, Canberra

Printed and bound in China

National Library of Australia

Cataloguing-in-Publication data

Bradford, Jenny, 1936-

Little book of wildflowers in silk ribbon.

Includes index.

ISBN 1 86351 227 6.

1. Silk ribbon embroidery. 2. Decoration and ornament -

Plant forms. I. Title. (Series : Milner craft series).

746.44

List of Flowers

HELPFUL HINTS FOR WORKING THE FLOWER DESIGNS

• All colour plates are printed the actual size of the original worked samples.

• Design details are listed in order of working.

• Reading the diagrams. Each new step is depicted by solid lines with previous steps shown in dotted lines.

Basic Requirements

• Always use a hoop for ribbon embroidery. All designs in this book were worked on a 9 cm (3½") spring tension hoop.

• Assorted chenille needles sizes 18 – 22 are recommended for ribbon embroidery (the eye of the needle should create a hole large enough to allow the ribbon to spread out easily) and crewel and straw needles for thread embroidery.

• Fabric. The samples have been worked on raw (noil) silk. Homespun, silk dupion, evenweave cotton or linen are all suitable materials.

• Try to work with a clear picture of the flower to help you with the interpretation. A fresh flower is ideal for this purpose but clear photographs or botanical drawings are often more accessible. See page 48 for a list of books used in preparing this book.

• Rough out the design on paper to clarify a picture in your mind. To transfer the design, using the minimum of markings on the fabric, start with the main stem lines where applicable and mark flower centres as required. I prefer a fine (0.5 mm) lead mechanical pencil such as a 'Pacer' for this purpose. No two people work ribbon exactly to the same tension, so it is better to mark as you go and not the complete design.

Silk Ribbon Requirements

All ribbon numbers are quoted from YLI silk ribbon colour card. Where applicable hand dyed ribbons are given as an alternative choice.

Various threads have been used for stems and stamens. DMC stranded threads may be substituted. One strand of DMC cotton equals one strand of Gumnut silk 'Stars' and is slightly thicker than the no. 50 threads used for stamens. Throughout the text the unidentified numbers are DMC threads.

Below is a list of the numbers, colours and thicknesses of ribbons used.

mm		2	4	7	13
3	white	★	★	★	★
7	pale pink		★	★	
13	soft yellow	★			
15	golden yellow	★			
20	bright green	★	★	★	
21	dark green		★		
23	mauve	★			
31	soft green	★	★		
32	blue green	★			
44	mid blue	★	★		
49	dark red	★	★		
52	old gold		★		
54	gold		★	★	
56	kaki	★			
60	mid lime green		★		
66	brown	★			
70	magenta		★		

mm		2	4	7	13
94	lime green		★		
99	royal blue		★		
101	lilac		★	★	
113	pinkie brown		★		
118	deep blue		★		
119	bright yellow	★	★	★	
125	pale blue	★			
128	deep pink		★		
140	brown	★			
146	bright magenta				★
153	pinkie red		★		
156	cream	★	★		
163	dusty pink		★		
170	light olive		★		
171	dark olive		★		
177	deep mauve		★	★	

$\mathcal{A}$USTRALIAN BLUEBELL

THREADS
644 beige grey
yellow No. 50 silk or rayon machine
*   embroidery thread*

RIBBONS
44 mid blue 2 mm & 4 mm
125 pale blue 2 mm
20 bright green 4 mm

Stems
Whipped chain, 2 strands 644
main stem, 1 strand for side stems

Flowers
Three straight stitch petals in 2
mm, 44. (1)

   Straight stitch centres in
machine embroidery thread (2)

   Two short straight stitch petals
in 2 mm, 125. (3)

   3 petal bells are worked in 2
mm 125, as shown in diagrams 1
and 4 on p. 10.

Buds
Double straight stitch in 4 mm,
44. ribbon.

Leaves
Ribbon stitch in 20.

BLUE TINSEL LILY

THREADS

3023 brown grey

White (PVA) adhesive

RIBBONS

20 bright green 2 mm
15 golden yellow 2 mm
118 deep blue 4 mm

Stems
Whipped chain, 2 strands 3023.

Leaves
Tight ribbon stitch in 20 worked from top of stem down.

Buds
Bullion lazy daisy in 118.

Flowers
Six petals in ribbon stitch 118 pulled semi-tight.

Stamens
Thread six short lengths of 2 mm yellow ribbon down through centre of the flower. Pin securely at the back. Moisten fingers with white glue and roll each ribbon end between your fingers to stiffen. Unpin ribbon ends at the back of the work and gently ease the stiffened ribbons down into the flower centre. Stitch ends securely at the back and trim. Trim stamens on the front to about 2 mm (1⁄16") in length.

$\mathcal{C}$ORREA

THREADS

*841 beige brown or silk 'Stars' 969
green flower correa — 906 & 907
pink flower correa — 712 & 3822*

RIBBONS

*green flower Rock correa — 21 dark
    green 4mm
60 mid lime green 4mm
94 lime green 4mm
pink flower Dusky Bells correa —
    20 bright green 4mm
163 dusty pink 4mm*

Stems
main stem — whipped chain, 2
strands 969 or 841.
side stems — 1 strand whipped
chain.

Flowers
In either 94 or 163 work outside
petals in bullion lazy daisy with
one wrap (one left hand and one
right hand stitch). Anchor petals
tipped outwards. (1)

Work four or five straight
stitches for stamens in 906 or
712 (2) and tip with a tiny straight
stitch in 907 or 3822. (3)

Complete flower with a
straight stitch worked from tip of
petal to base of flower in 94 or
163. (4)

Work a straight stitch across
the base of the flower in 60 or 20
to finish. (5)

Leaves
Straight stitch in 21 or 20.

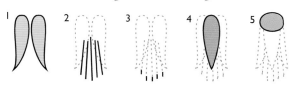

$\mathcal{C}$UT LEAF DAISY

THREADS
469 avocado green or silk 'Stars' 589
725 gold or silk 'Stars' 746

RIBBONS
23 mauve 2 mm

Greenery
Work network of stems in fly stitch in green cotton or silk.

Flowers
Mark small circle for centre (1) and work petals in 23 in straight stitch. (2 & 3)

Fill centres with colonial knots using 1 strand of gold cotton or silk.

Buds
Double straight stitch in 23 with fly stitch around base in green cotton or silk.

$\mathcal{E}$RIOSTEMON — WAX FLOWER

THREADS
White

RIBBONS
3 white 4 mm
20 bright green 4 mm
113 pinkie brown 4 mm
31 soft green 2 mm

Leaves
Long straight and ribbon stitch in 20. (1)

Flowers
See diagram 1 on p. 26 for stitch placement.

Five petal ribbon stitch in 3.

Centres
Colonial knot in 31. Using a fine needle (no. 8 or 9 straw needle) and one strand of white cotton, work colonial knots around the upper edge of the ribbon knot.

Buds
Two straight stitches in 113, one directly over the other for each bud. (2) Stitch a straight stitch in 20 across the base of each bud. (3)

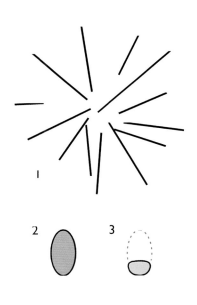

$\mathscr{F}$AIRY FAN FLOWER

THREADS
801 coffee brown
3822 gold or silk 'Stars' 708

RIBBONS
70 magenta 4 mm
21 dark green 4 mm
52 old gold 4 mm, (or Kacoonda 106)

Stems
Whipped chain, 2 strands 801.

Leaves
Straight stitch, clustered and over-lapping in 21.

Flowers
Five petals, fan shape, worked in 70 in ribbon stitch. (1)

Tiny straight stitches in 708 onto base of petals (2)

Rolled ribbon stitch worked in 52 across the base of the petals. (Leave tiny roll of ribbon against yellow stitching instead of pulling ribbon right through to the back.) (3)

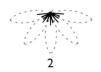

I   2   3

ℱLANNEL FLOWER

THREADS
Gumnut Daisies 624 soft green

RIBBONS
31 soft green 2 mm
31 soft green 4 mm
156 cream 4 mm

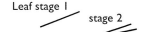

Leaf stage 1
stage 2

1

Stem with leaves

2

Stems
Whipped chain, 1 strand 624.

Leaves
Straight stitch with a fly
stitch, 1 strand 624. (1 & 2)

Bud
3 or 4 ribbon stitches in 156.
4 straight stitches into lower
half of petals.

Flowers
Mark circle for centre of flower 6
mm (¼") diameter.

Work bullion lazy daisy petals
with two wraps for each bullion in
156. Anchor some stitches off line
to create movement. (3)

Using 2 mm 31 fill centre with
colonial knots.

Using 4 mm 31 back stitch
over the tips of each
petal. (4)

3

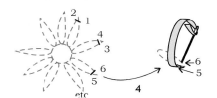

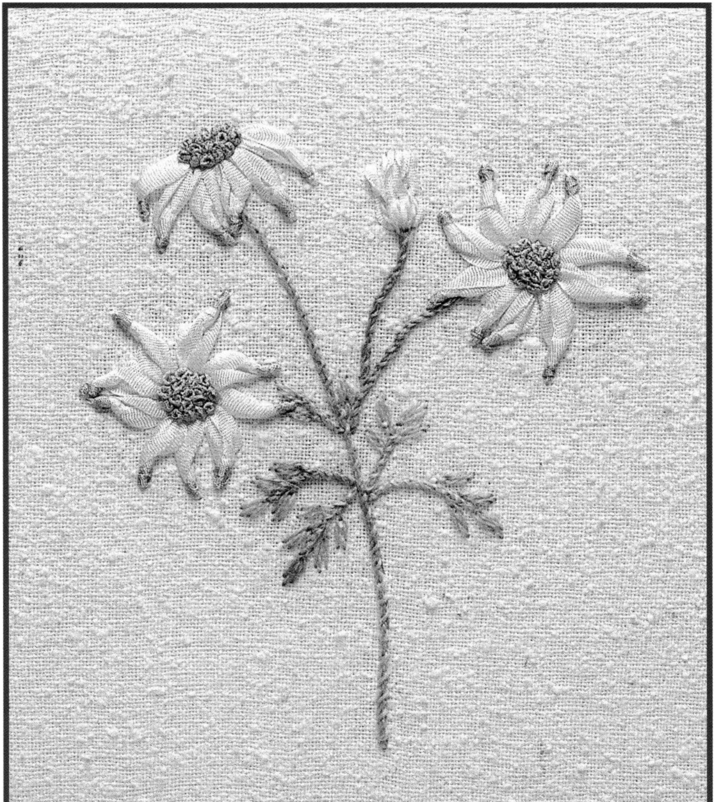

$\mathcal{G}$UM LEAVES & NUTS

THREAD
523 fern green
918 red copper

RIBBON
32 blue green 2 mm
66 brown 2 mm
Mill Hill pebble beads for nuts
(black or clear)

Draw leaf shape on to fabric.

Stems
Whipped chain, 2 strands 523. Highlight down one side only in stem stitch using 1 strand 918.

Leaf
Fill in leaves in straight stitch using 32, starting with a stitch about 1.5 cm (⅝") long at the tip of the leaf. Spread ribbon carefully to prevent rolling at the edges. Space stitches

carefully to cover the fabric but not overlap too much.

Couch leaf outline in 918 and centre vein in 523.

Wrap beads with 66 leaving tails of ribbon for attaching to work. Bring both ends of ribbon together at one end of the bead and wrap firmly with a single strand of 918 to form a stalk. Thread ends to the back of the work, adjust length and sew securely.

$\mathcal{H}$OVEA (MAUVE) & NATIVE GORSE (YELLOW)

THREADS

Hovea — 420 hazelnut brown or silk
  'Stars' 948
Native Gorse — 523 fern green or
  silk 'Stars' 586
no. 50 silk or rayon thread in red

RIBBONS

Hovea — 177 deep mauve 7 mm &
  4 mm (or Kacoonda 109)
3 white 2 mm
  20 bright green 4 mm
Native Gorse — 54 gold 7 mm
  (or Kacoonda 103)
49 dark red 2 mm
171 dark olive 4 mm

Stems

Whipped chain, 2 strands of thread.

Flowers

Two stitches in 7 mm looped
straight stitch. (1)

Hovea — two tiny straight stitches in 3. (a)

Gorse — three or four
straight stitches in red
thread into each petal.
(a)

Hovea — two looped
straight stitches in 4mm
177 at base of white
stitches.(b)

Gorse — one small ribbon stitch
in 49, in centre, with two looped
straight stitches to form an arc
over the ribbon stitch. (b)

Buds

Double straight stitch in 54.
Straight stitch in 171 to cover
lower half of bud.

Leaves

Hovea — longer
straight stitches in
20.

Gorse — short
ribbon stitches in
171.

Hovea (a)

Hovea (b)

Gorse (a)

Gorse (b)

THREAD
White

RIBBON
3 white 13 mm & 4 mm
21 dark green 4 mm

Use a stiletto or bradawl to make holes for flower petals. A size 13 needle is recommended for 13 mm ribbon.

Flowers
4 looped petals in white 13 mm ribbon. Stitch down with a straight stitch using a single strand of thread.

Colonial knot in white 4 mm for centre.

Buds
Double straight stitch in 13 mm. 3 ribbon stitches in 21 to cover lower third of white stitches.

Stamens
Thread needle with 4 strands of white cotton and pass from front to back next to edge of colonial knot. Backstitch threads at back of work and return needle to front close to start. Cut threads. Repeat around the centre knot 5 or 6 times. Brush ends and trim to about 4 mm (³⁄₁₆") long then lightly touch tips with brown marker pen to tint.

Leaves
Long straight stitches in 21.

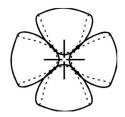

$\mathcal{N}$ATIVE FLAX AND COMMON BUTTERCUP

THREADS
Flax — silk 'Stars' 644 olive green
Buttercup — silk 'Stars' 589 soft green & 746 gold

RIBBONS
Flax — 44 mid blue 4 mm
20 bright green 4 mm
13 soft yellow 2mm
Buttercups — 54 gold 4mm
20 bright green 2 mm
31 soft green 2mm

Stems
Whipped chain, 1 strand 644 or 589.

Flowers
Work 5-petal flowers in straight stitch in 44 or 54. Leave stitches on flax flowers slightly looped. Leave a slightly larger centre for buttercups. (1)

Buds
Buttercup buds are 3 straight stitches in 54 and finished with 3 small stitches in 20, 2 mm.

Work flax buds with one or two straight stitches (second stitch directly over first stitch) in 44. Finish with fly stitch in 644 thread.

Leaves
Straight stitches, some couched, in 20.

Flower centres
Single colonial knot in 13 or 31. For buttercup add colonial knots in single strand 746 thread around the ribbon knot.

Flax or buttercup flowers

Buttercup buds

Flax buds

$\mathcal{N}$ATIVE LASIANDRA

RIBBONS
15 golden yellow 2 mm
146 bright magenta 7mm
Spark organdie olive green 9 mm

White (PVA) adhesive

Flowers
6 petals in 146 around a small
centre. Work a colonial knot in 15
in centre (size 18 chenille needle)
and add stiffened ribbon stamens
as below.

Stamens
Cut a piece of 15, 7 cm (2¾")
long, fold in half. Thread the
looped end of the ribbon into the
needle (size 22 chenille) and pull
to the back of the work through

the centre of the knot. Pin loop to
hold securely. On right side, put a
dab of white glue on each ribbon
and roll between finger and thumb
(do not get glue on the very end
of the ribbon). Fray ends of ribbon and trim, then pull stamens
down to required length and
secure ribbon at the back of the
work with fine thread.

Leaves
Straight stitch in spark organdie.

ℕODDING BLUE LILY

THREADS
3347 yellow green

RIBBONS
15 golden yellow 2 mm
20 bright green 4 mm & 7 mm
99 royal blue 4 mm
Spark organdie olive green in 5mm

Stems
Stitch upper leaves in 7 mm 20 before working stems in whipped chain with a single strand of 3347.

Flowers
Work in ribbon stitch using 99 in order shown, passing needle down through ribbon off centre to angle petals 3 and 4 slightly. Work stamens in very tight ribbon stitch in 15.

Buds
Straight stitch in 4 mm 99 overlaid with a second stitch in spark organdie. Fly stitch around base of bud with two strands cotton.

Leaves
Add couched twisted ribbon stitch leaves in 20 at base of stem.

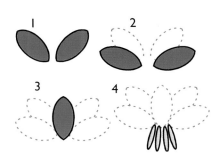

ℛED BORONIA

THREADS
3348 yellow green & 918 red copper

RIBBONS
153 pinkie red 4 mm
20 bright green 2 mm

Stems
Whipped chain, 2 strands green thread.

Leaves
Tight ribbon stitch worked in 20 from top to bottom of the stem.

Flowers
Work 2 small bullion lazy daisy stitches in 153 with one wrap side by side. (1) Centre a ribbon stitch over the first two stitches. (2)

Attach flowers to stems with small fly stitches in a single strand of brown cotton. (3)

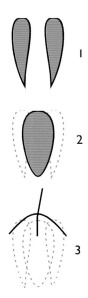

$\mathcal{S}$UMMER STAR FLOWERS

THREADS

3072 beaver grey
no. 50 silk or rayon thread in bright
* yellow and soft green*

RIBBONS

20 bright green 2 mm
119 bright yellow 2 mm & 4 mm

Stems
Whipped chain, 2 strands 3072.

Buds
Double straight stitch using 119 in 4 mm. Use green silk to finish buds as shown.

Bud base — One straight stitch with fly stitch around the bud in soft green silk thread. (a)

Upper part of bud — One extended fly stitch (b) with two extra straight stitches from the bud tip. (c)

Flowers
See diagram 1 on p. 26 for stitch placement.

5 petals in ribbon stitch in 119, 4 mm finished with colonial knot centre in 119, 2 mm. Work pistil stitch stamens around the centre in no. 50 thread.

Leaves
Ribbon stitch using 20 pulled very tight to form needle like leaves.

bud

b

a

c

TREE ORCHID (WHITE), COOKTOWN ORCHID (PINK)

THREAD
3347 yellow green

RIBBON
Tree Orchid — 3 white 7 mm
  & 4 mm
128 deep pink in 4 mm
Cooktown Orchid — 7 pale pink
  7 mm & 4 mm
49 dark red 4 mm

Stems
Whipped chain, 2 strands 3347.

Flowers
Two side petals in 7 mm, straight
stitch. (1)

Three smaller petals in 4 mm
matching, ribbon stitch. (2)

Centres — small straight stitch
in 128 or 49 4 mm. (2)

Two small looped straight
stitches in 4 mm pink 128 or 7
ribbon to form hood over the
straight stitch centre. One longer
looped petal for base of throat in
white for Tree Orchid or pink for
Cooktown Orchid. (3)

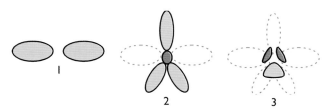

Waratah

THREADS
471 avocado green

RIBBONS
White version — 170 light olive
*   4 mm*
156 cream 2 mm

56 kaki 2 mm (or Kacoonda 8E)
140 brown 2 mm
Red version — 49 dark red 2 mm &
*   4 mm*
140 brown 2 mm
Spark organdie 9 mm olive green

Stems
Whipped chain in 2 mm 140.

Flowers
Work 2 mm ribbon colonial knot cluster. (1) Cover each knot with a straight stitch. (2) On the white version, use 170 for 3 or 4 centre knots.

Work 3 more knots in centre front (3) and cover with longer straight stitches. (4)

Work base petals in bullion lazy daisy (2 wraps) in 4 mm ribbon. (5)

Finish with pistil stitches in 2 mm ribbon filling in area between cone and lower petals. (6)

Leaves
Double straight stitch in spark organdie, and single straight stitch vein up centre in single strand of cotton.

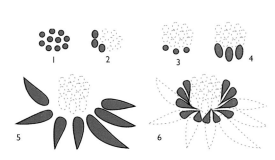

ᒍ ELLOW AND PURPLE FLAG

THREADS
Yellow — 725 topaz
Purple — white

RIBBONS
*Yellow — 119 bright yellow in 7 mm
    or 4 mm*
Purple — 101 lilac in 7mm or 4 mm
Both — 32 blue green in 2 mm

Leaves
Clustered straight and ribbon stitches in 32, twisted or folded and couched to form bent leaves.

Flowers
Make a hole with a very large (no. 13) needle or stiletto for flower centre. Start straight stitch petals at outer tip and take needle down through centre hole carefully.

Stitch length should be 5-7 mm ($\frac{3}{16}$" – $\frac{1}{4}$") for 7 mm ribbon or 3-4 mm ($\frac{1}{8}$" – $\frac{3}{16}$") for 4 mm ribbon.

Centres — using two strands of cotton, 3 colonial knots for 7 mm flowers or 3 french knots for 4 mm flowers.

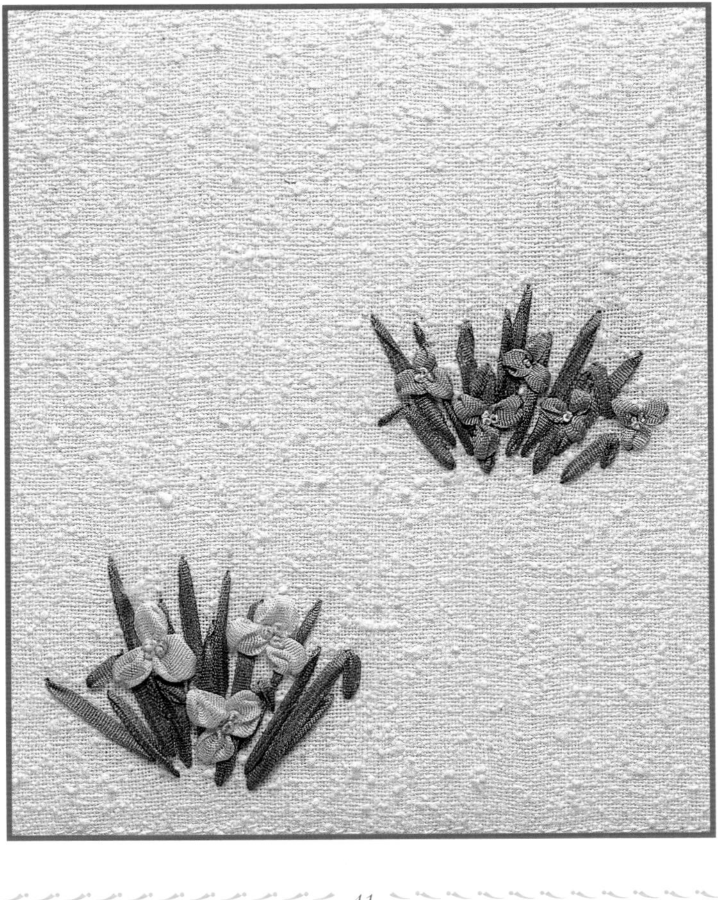

Stitch Glossary

On all stitch and flower diagrams the odd numbers refer to the needle passing up through the fabric from back to front. The even numbers refer to the needle passing down through the fabric from the front to the back.

Flower sizes may be altered by changing ribbon width and revising stitch size in proportion.

BULLION LAZY DAISY

Keep ribbon flat and smooth at all times. Pull firmly to tighten the stitch and fine down the tip of the petal.

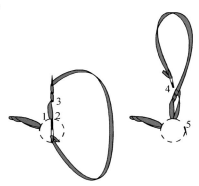

COLONIAL KNOTS

Hold ribbon in the left hand and, pointing the needle away from you, hook it under the ribbon from left to right.

Turn the needle anti-clockwise over the ribbon to hook under the ribbon held by the left hand.

The needle direction is reversed back over the ribbon and passed to the back of the fabric at point 2.

Not shown, but essential, is to pull down gently on the ribbon held in the left hand, to ensure that the knot is resting on the fabric as the needle is passed through the fabric.

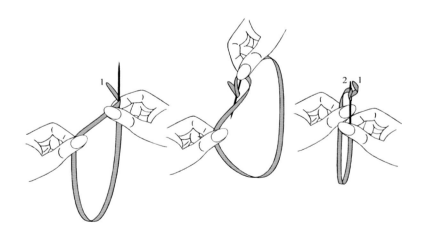

FEATHER STITCH

This is a 'one way' stitch. Take care that all the stems point in the right direction on a design.

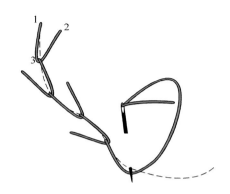

FLY STITCH

Bring the needle up at 1, then down at 2 and out again at 3. Keep the thread from point 1 looped under the needle at 3 and pull the needle through.

Anchor the stitch by passing the needle to the back of the work at 4. A stem can be created by moving point 4 further away from point 3.

PISTIL STITCH

Bring the needle up at point 1 and pick up the thread once or twice around the needle. Return the needle to the back of the work the required distance from point 1, pulling the thread taut around the needle as it is passed through the fabric.

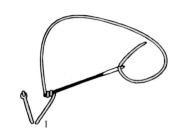

RIBBON STITCH

Always spread the ribbon carefully and pull the ribbon very gently to complete the stitch.

STRAIGHT STITCH FLAT

Always spread the ribbon and gently tighten the stitch to the desired tension.

STRAIGHT OR RIBBON STITCH TWISTED (COUCHED)

Always spread the ribbon and gently tighten the stitch to the desired tension.

Use matching embroidery thread to anchor the ribbon with a couching thread as you fold the ribbon to change direction.

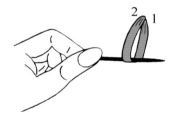

STRAIGHT STITCH LOOPED

Always spread the ribbon and take care not to disturb and distort the stitches as you work.

WHIPPED CHAIN

Work a base line of chain stitch then, using a tapestry needle, whip back up the line of stitches working into each chain but not through the fabric.

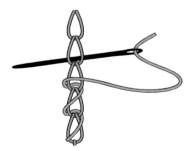

More detailed instructions for these stitches (except whipped chain) can be found in my other books *Original Designs for Silk Ribbon Embroidery* and *Jenny Bradford Embroidery Collection*

ACKNOWLEDGMENTS

I would like to thank Alan & Margaret Linklater of Cotton On Creations for supplying the ribbons and Julie Ellis of Gumnuts for the silk 'Stars' thread used in this book.

My thanks to Sally Milner for inviting me to contribute to this charming series of books.

Finally, as always, there would be no book without my husband Don's support and expertise in drawing the diagrams, doing all the necessary computer work (I remain computer illiterate) and careful proof reading.

BIBLIOGRAPHY

Denise Greig *The Australian Gardener's Wildflower Catalogue* Angus & Robertson

Leonard Cronin *The Concise Australian Flora* Reed Books

Stirling Macoboy *What Flower Is That?* Lansdowne Press

Rica Erikson, A.S.George, N.G.Marchant, M.K.Morcombe *Flowers & Plants of Western Australia* Reed Books

Nan & Hugh Nicholson *Australian Rainforest Plants III & IV* Terania Rainforest Publishing